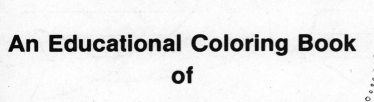

An Educational Coloring Book of
WHALES

EDITOR
Linda Spizzirri

ASST. EDITOR
Jacqueline Sontheimer

COPY REFERENCE
Museums of
Natural History

ILLUSTRATION
Peter M. Spizzirri
Claire Vanderslice

COVER ART
Peter M. Spizzirri

CONTENTS

An Educational Coloring Book of WHALES • Published by SPIZZIRRI PUBLISHING CO., INC., P.O. BOX 664 MEDINAH, ILLINOIS 60157. No part of this publication may be reproduced by any means without the express written consent of the publisher. All national and international rights reserved on the entire contents of this publication.
Printed in U.S.A.

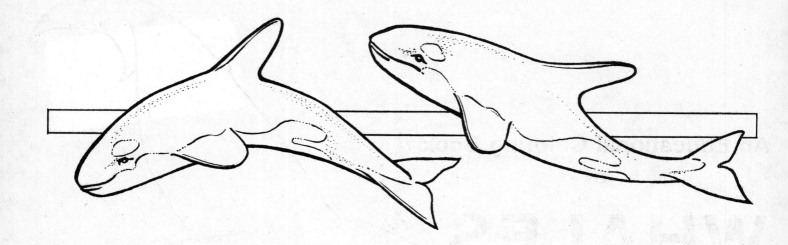

NAME:	BLUE WHALE (*Balaennoptera musculus*)
WHERE IT LIVES:	NORTHERN ATLANTIC AND PACIFIC
SIZE:	LENGTH: 70 TO 100 FEET WEIGHT: 150 TO 200 TONS
WHAT IT EATS:	KRILL (PLANKTONIC ORGANISMS)
COLOR IT:	BLUISH GRAY TO BLUISH BLACK, UNDER SIDE LIGHT PATCHES OF VARYING COLOR
INTERESTING FACTS:	Even in prehistoric times, nothing grew to the size of the blue whale. It is the largest living mammal in the world. The whaling industry has killed without regard for the future life of this whale. The blue whale is an endangered species today. About 1500 whales exist in the north Pacific and a few hundred in the north Atlantic. A single calf is born every two years, and many zoologist fear the blue whale cannot recover from being over hunted.

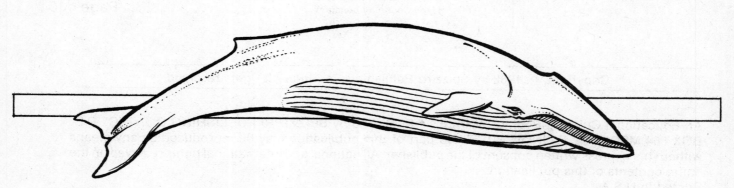

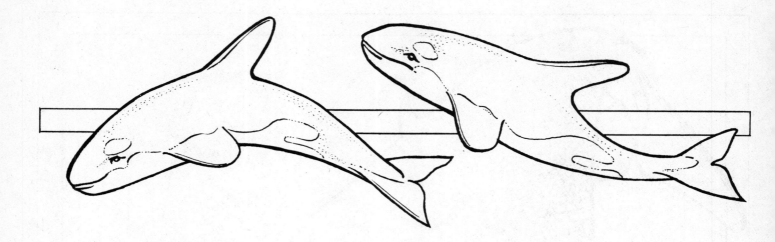

NAME:	NARWHAL (*Monodon monoceros*)
WHERE IT LIVES:	ARCTIC SEAS, ALONG COASTS AND SOMETIMES IN RIVERS
SIZE:	LENGTH: 13 TO 15 FEET WEIGHT: 2000 TO 3500 POUNDS
WHAT IT EATS:	CRUSTACEANS, SQUID AND FISH
COLOR IT:	BROWNISH UPPER PARTS, WHITISH UNDER PARTS, MOTTLED SPOTTING OVER THE ENTIRE BODY
INTERESTING FACTS:	The narwhal comprises a single species. It is unique because the male grows a tusk from its upper jaw. This tusk is a lancelike hollow spiral growing to 9 feet in length. In medieval times the narwhals tusk were regarded as the "horn of the unicorn", and traded to Europeans by the Norsemen. Narwhals make a shrill whistling sound when exhaling after a dive. The mother makes a deep roaring sound when calling her young.

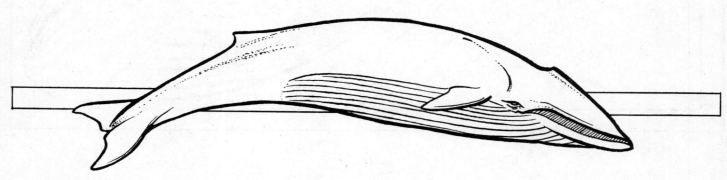

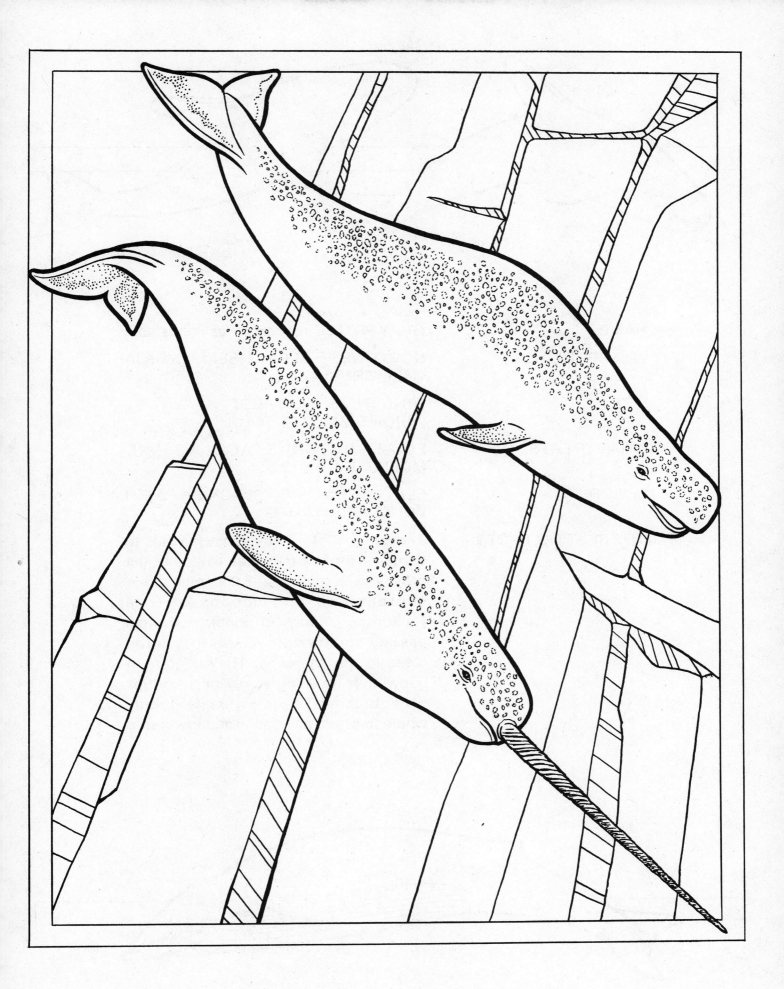

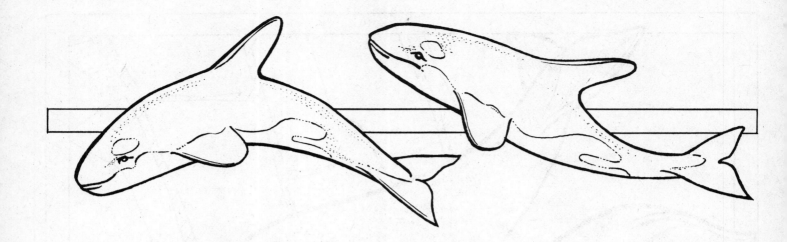

NAME:	GRAY WHALE (*Eschrichtius robustus*)
WHERE IT LIVES:	NORTHWEST BERING SEA TO BAJA CALIFORNIA
SIZE:	LENGTH: 46 TO 48 FEET WEIGHT: 25 TO 35 TONS
WHAT IT EATS:	FLOATING CRUSTACEANS AND MOLLUSKS
COLOR IT:	SLATE GRAY TO BLACKISH WITH WHITE SPLOTCHES
INTERESTING FACTS:	The gray whale is the most familiar to people in the United States. Annually, the gray whale makes a 5,000 mile polar migration to the lagoons of Baja California. Millions of people see them passing southward because they travel close to the shoreline. They migrate in midwinter, traveling singly or in groups of two or three. The gray whale is the only whale to breed and calf in shallow water.

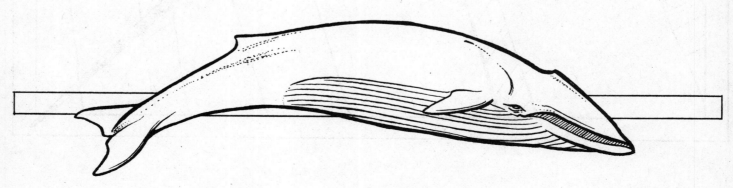

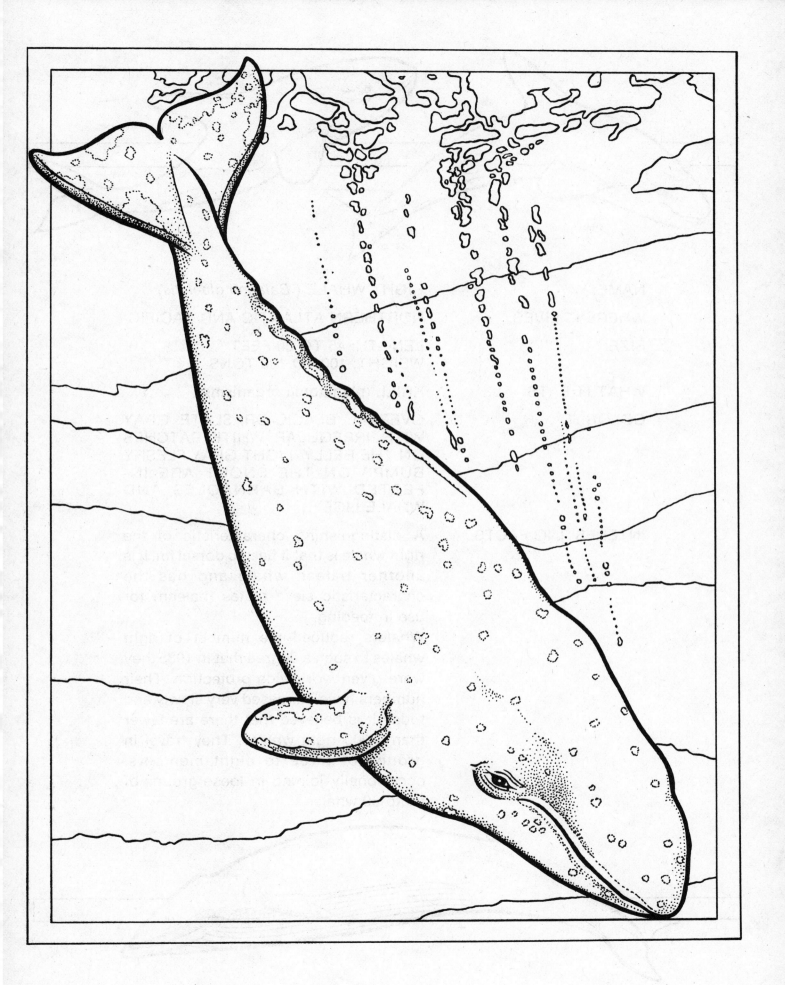

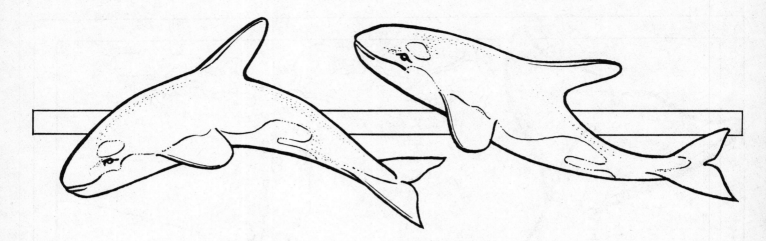

NAME:	RIGHT WHALE (*Balaena glacialis*)
WHERE IT LIVES:	NORTHERN ATLANTIC AND PACIFIC
SIZE:	LENGTH: 45 TO 60 FEET WEIGHT: 100 TO 120 TONS
WHAT IT EATS:	KRILL (planktonic organisms)
COLOR IT:	OVERALL BLACK OR SLATE GRAY WITH IRREGULAR WHITE PATCHES ON THE BELLY. LIGHT GRAY FLESHY BUMPS ON THE SNOUT ARE INFESTED WITH BARNACLES AND WHALE LICE
INTERESTING FACTS:	A distinguishing characteristic of the right whale is that it has no dorsal fin. It is another baleen whale and has the characteristic sieve plates (baleen) for use in feeding. Whalers reduced the number of right whales to such a degree that in 1935 they were given worldwide protection. Their numbers have increased very slowly and today it is believed that there are fewer than 1,000 right whales. They travel in groups of three to eight members, occasionally joining in loose groups of up to 30 whales.

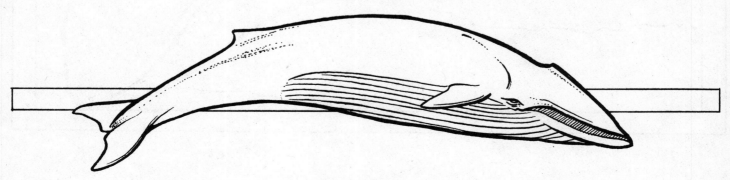

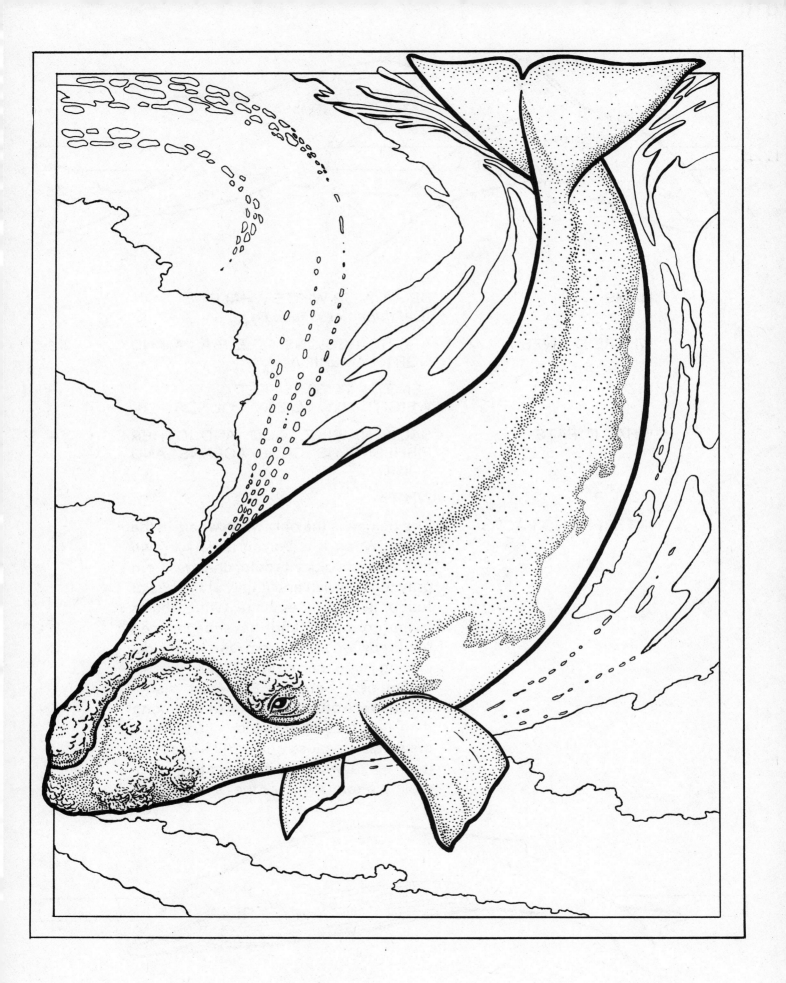

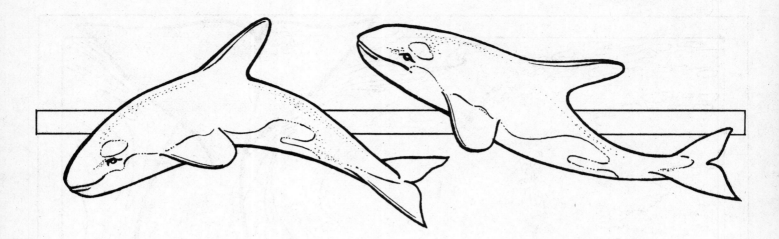

NAME:	BELUGA OR WHITE WHALE (*Delphinapterus leucas*)
WHERE IT LIVES:	ARCTIC REGIONS OF EURASIA AND NORTH AMERICA
SIZE:	LENGTH: 14 TO 15 FEET WEIGHT: 3000 TO 3200 POUNDS
WHAT IT EATS:	SALMON, PIKE, COD AND OTHER FISHES PLUS CRUSTACEANS AND SQUID
COLOR IT:	WHITE
INTERESTING FACTS:	The beluga is the only white whale in the world. When it is born it is dark brown and as it gets older its color changes from gray to yellowish and finally at the age of four or five becomes white. White whales swim up rivers and have been seen hundreds of miles from salt water. At calving time more than 1,000 whales gather near Canada's Somerset Island. Belugas are often heard "talking" among themselves as their voices carry above the water. Because of the trill like sound they make when communicating, they are often referred to as the "sea canary."

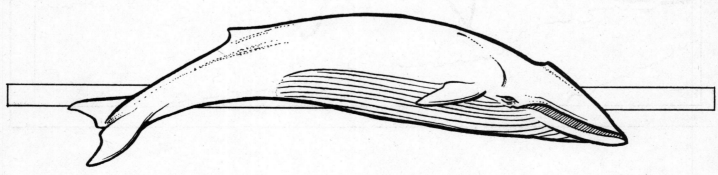

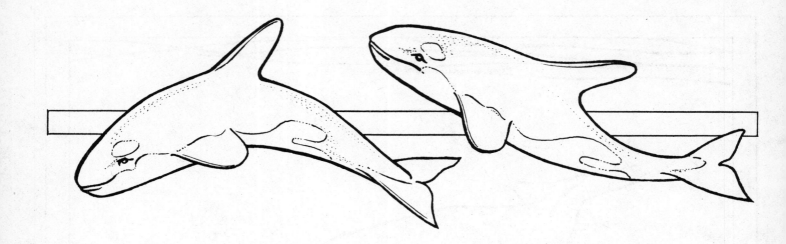

NAME:	SPERM WHALE (*Physeter catodon*)
WHERE IT LIVES:	IN THE OCEANS OF BOTH THE NORTH AND SOUTH HEMISPHERES
SIZE:	LENGTH: 41 TO 60 FEET WEIGHT: 26 TO 63 TONS
WHAT IT EATS:	SQUID, OCTOPUS AND DEEP WATER FISHES
COLOR IT:	GRAY BELLY, DARK BLUISH GRAY BODY, BLACK BACK, FINS AND TAIL
INTERESTING FACTS:	Today, the sperm whale is the most abundant of all the great whales. These whales usually travel in schools of 15 to 20 members. When migrating, they join into groups of several hundred. Mating probably occurs in warm waters and the young are born 12 to 16 months later. The newborn calf, which is about 13 feet long and weighs about 1 ton, is nursed for at least 6 months.

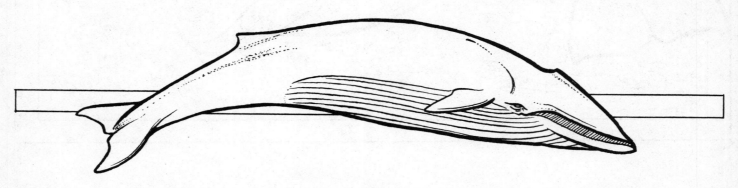

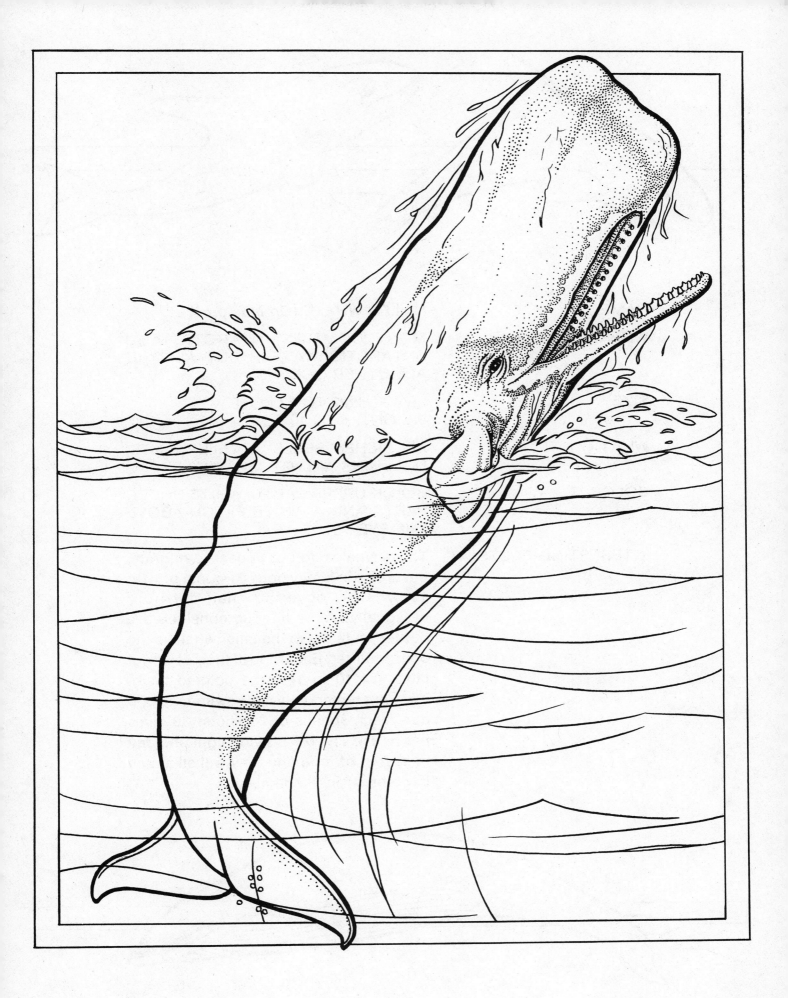

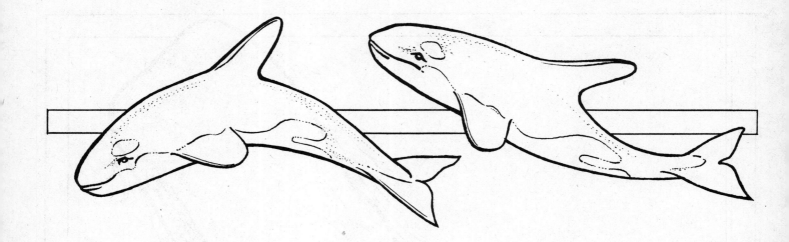

NAME:	KILLER WHALE (*Orcinus orca*)
WHERE IT LIVES:	MOST COMMON IN ARCTIC AND ANTARCTIC WATERS BUT ALSO IN ALL OTHER OCEANS
SIZE:	LENGTH: 22 TO 32 FEET WEIGHT: 5 TO 10 TONS
WHAT IT EATS:	ALL FISHES, SEALS, SEA ELEPHANTS, DOLPHINS AND OTHER WHALES
COLOR IT:	BLACK UPPER PARTS, WHITE UNDER PARTS AND A WHITE PATCH ABOVE THE EYE
INTERESTING FACTS:	These whales do not appear to migrate, but cruise in family pods (groups) of 10 to 15 whales, covering their territory seasonally. As a tiger is considered a hunter on land, so the killer whale is the ocean hunter. Each side of their powerful jaws has 10 to 14 large pointed teeth. They are remarkably agile swimmers that can reach speeds of 26 knots (30 miles per hour). The pods swim night and day in search of food and they will all attack large prey simultaneously.

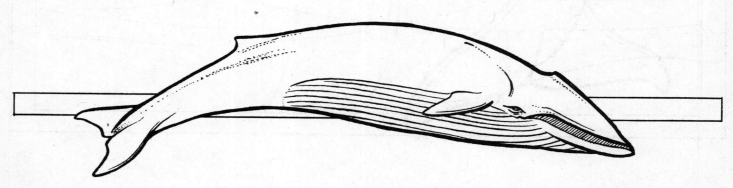

14

NAME:	HUMPBACK WHALE (*Megaptera novaeangliae*)
WHERE IT LIVES:	ATLANTIC AND PACIFIC OCEANS
SIZE:	LENGTH: ABOUT 50 FEET WEIGHT: 50 TONS
WHAT IT EATS:	KRILL (PLANKTONIC ORGANISMS) AND SMALL FISH
COLOR IT:	BLACKISH ABOVE WITH A WHITE THROAT AND BREAST
INTERESTING FACTS:	One of the most outstanding features of this whale is that its flippers are 14 feet long. Humpback whales often have many barnacles and whale lice patches on their heads and bodies. These slow moving friendly whales inhabit warm waters during the winter and migrate north and south to polar waters in the summer. Only a few thousand humpback whales exist today because they too have been victims of overhunting.

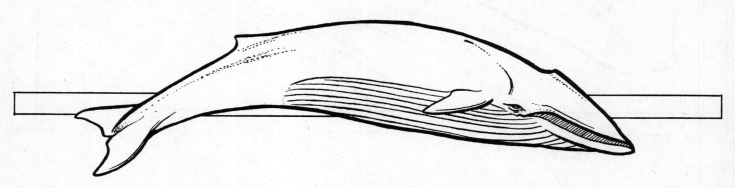

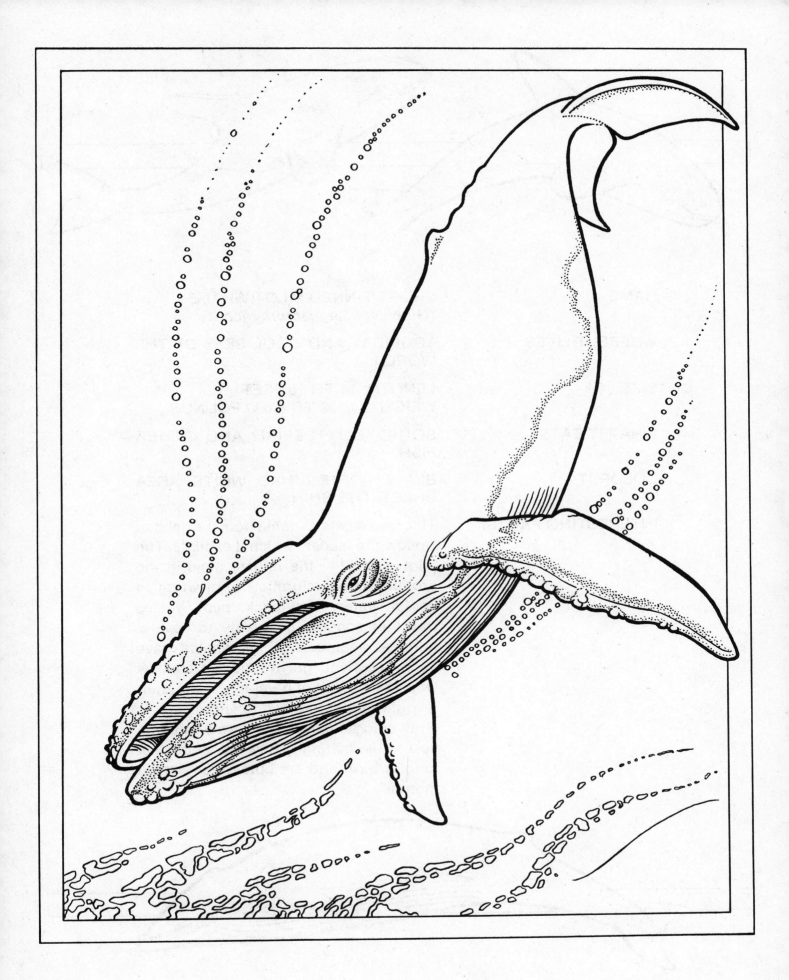

NAME:	SHORT-FINNED PILOT WHALE (*Globicephala macrorhynchus*)
WHERE IT LIVES:	TROPICAL AND COOL SEAS OF THE WORLD
SIZE:	LENGTH: 14 TO 20 FEET WEIGHT: 4,000 TO 6,000 POUNDS
WHAT IT EATS:	SQUID, CUTTLEFISH AND OTHER FISH
COLOR IT:	BLACK; OFTEN HAS WHITE AREA UNDER THE CHIN
INTERESTING FACTS:	This whale gets its name from the habit of "follow the leader" which it exhibits. The pilot is usually the largest male in the group. During migration from warm to cooler waters and back, pilot whales travel in schools of twenty to several hundred members. Pilot whales have been known to get trapped in shallow water as a result of pursuing squid, their favorite food, too close to shore. Gray colored calves are born about one year after mating. They are eight feet long at birth and are nursed for sixteen months.

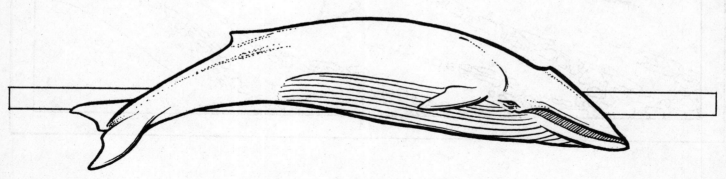

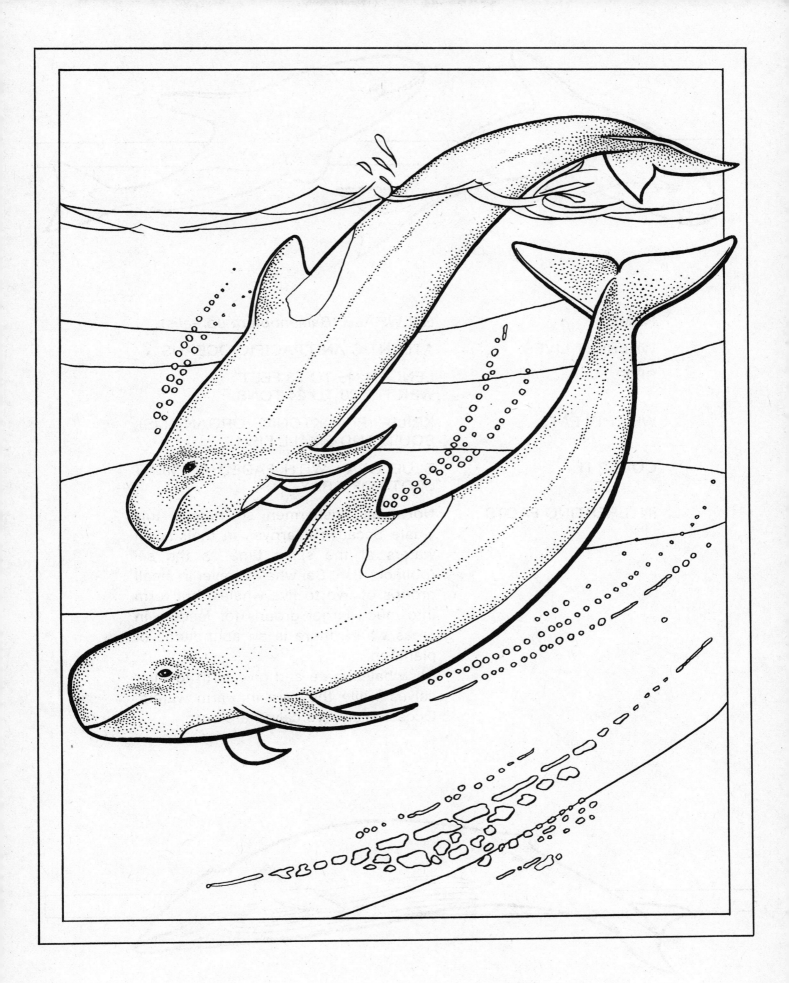

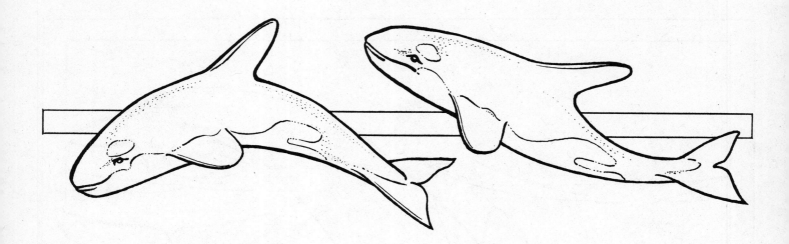

NAME:	SEI WHALE (*Balaenoptera borealis*)
WHERE IT LIVES:	ATLANTIC AND PACIFIC OCEANS
SIZE:	LENGTH: 45 TO 53 FEET WEIGHT: 20 TO 24 TONS
WHAT IT EATS:	KRILL (PLANKTONIC ORGANISMS), SQUID AND SMALL FISH
COLOR IT:	BLUE GRAY WITH FADED PIGMENT SPOTS OF GRAY
INTERESTING FACTS:	Norwegian fishermen so named this whale because it arrives in their coast waters at the same time as the sei (pollack) fish. Sei whales travel in small groups of two to five whales, but form into much larger groups for feeding in areas where there is an abundance of plankton. Sei whales mate and give birth to their calves while they are in warm waters. Occasionally two calves are born.

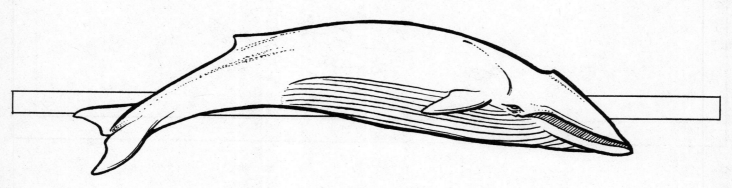

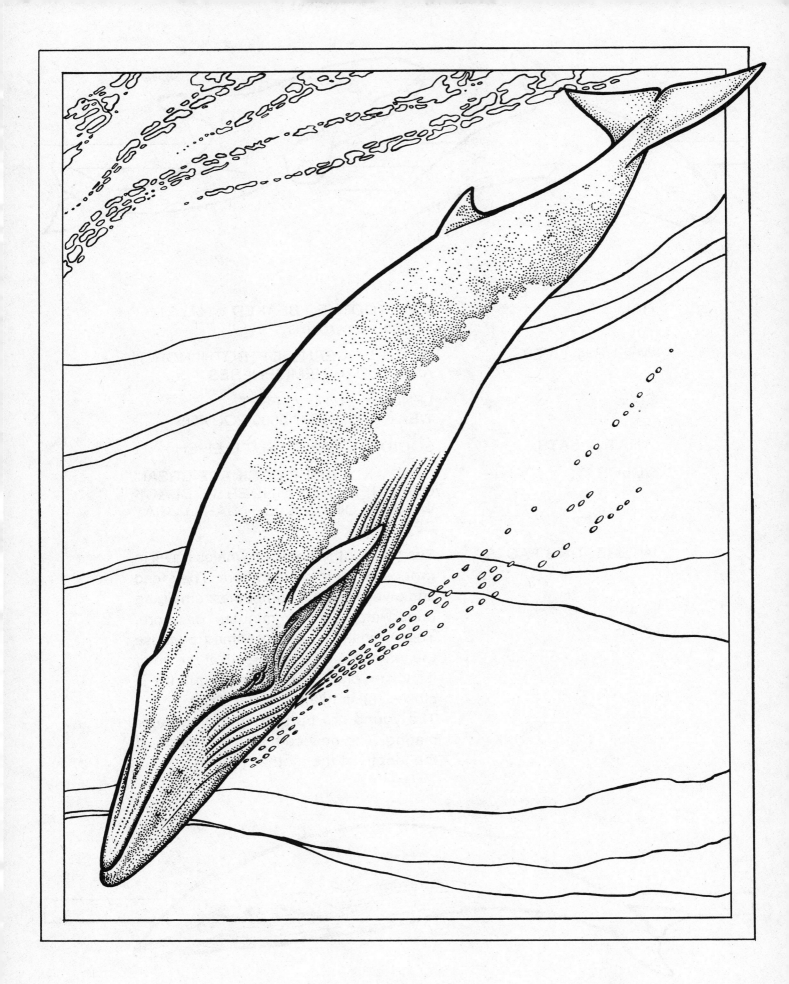

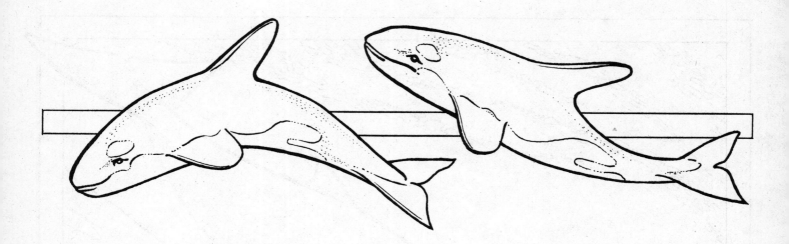

NAME:	TWO-TOOTHED BEAKED WHALE (*Ziphius cavirostris*)
WHERE IT LIVES:	IN THE OCEANS OF BOTH NORTH AND SOUTH HEMISPHERES
SIZE:	LENGTH: 21 TO 28 FEET WEIGHT: 3500 TO 6500 POUNDS
WHAT IT EATS:	SQUID, OCTOPUS, CUTTLEFISH
COLOR IT:	FACE AND UPPER BACK ARE CREAM COLORED, REMAINDER IS BLACK WITH BLOTCHES OF DARK GRAY BELOW
INTERESTING FACTS:	The two-toothed beaked whales travel in groups of 30 to 40 members. They feed and dive in groups, sometimes remaining underwater for 30 minutes or more. These whales were so named because the male whale has two teeth at the tip of its lower jaw. Even when its mouth is closed these two teeth stand out. The young are born about 1 year after mating. The new calf is about one third the length of the mother (7 feet).

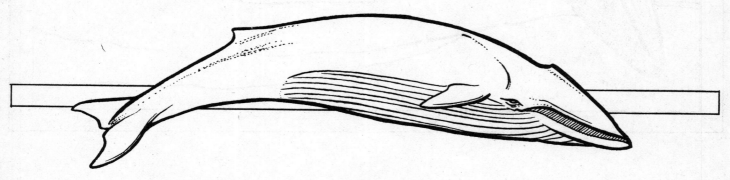

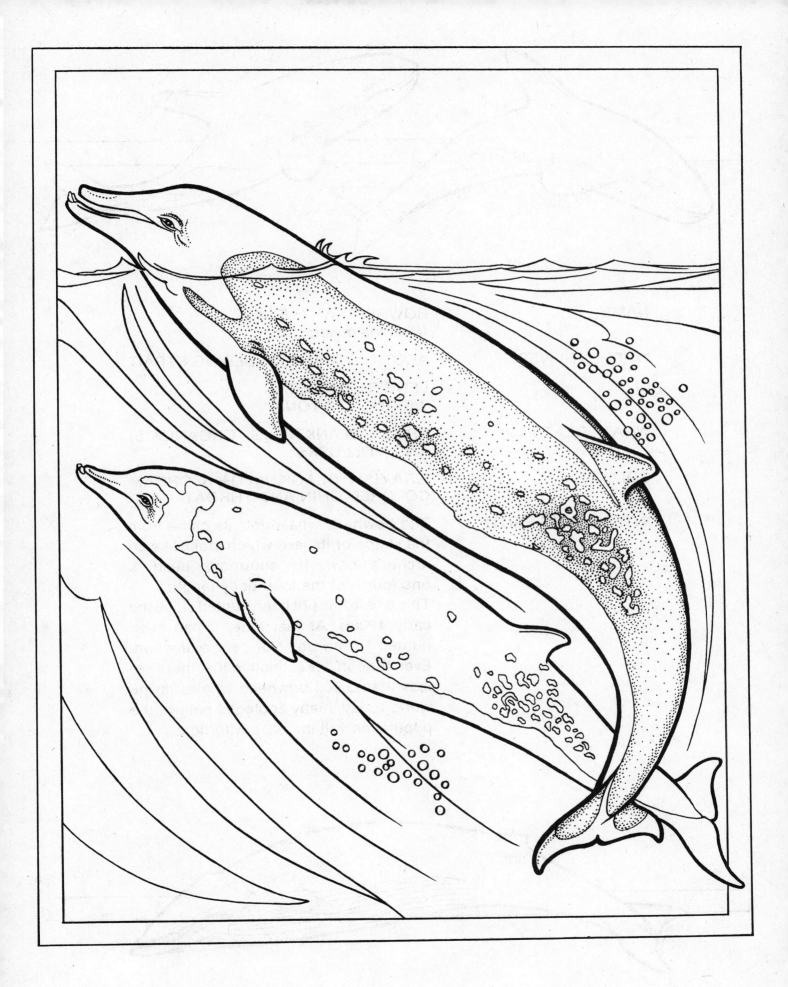

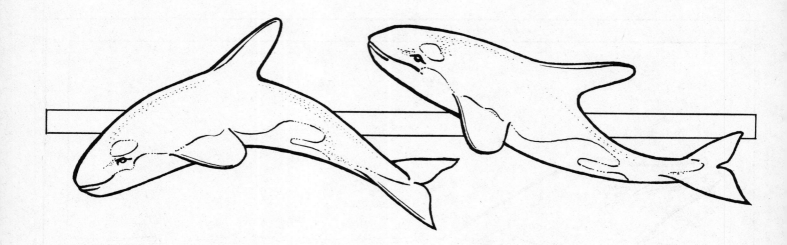

NAME:	BOWHEAD WHALE (*Balaena mysticetus*)
WHERE IT LIVES:	ARCTIC OCEAN AND BERING STRAIT
SIZE:	LENGTH: 60 FEET WEIGHT: 100 TONS
WHAT IT EATS:	KRILL (PLANKTONIC ORGANISMS) AND MOLLUSKS
COLOR IT:	GRAYISH BLACK WITH A CREAM COLORED CHIN AND THROAT
INTERESTING FACTS:	The bowhead whale gets its name from the shape of its jaw, which looks like an archer's bow. Its enormous head is one fourth of the total body length. This whale has not been hunted since the early 1900's. At that time, it had been hunted to the point of near extinction. Even though it is estimated that there are less than 3,000 bowhead whales in the world today, many zoologist believe the population will increase with time.

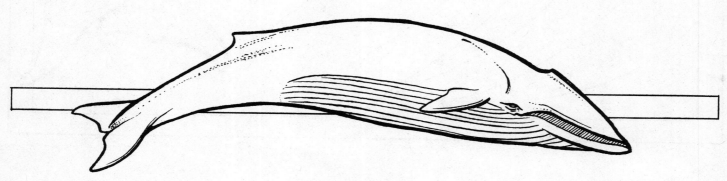

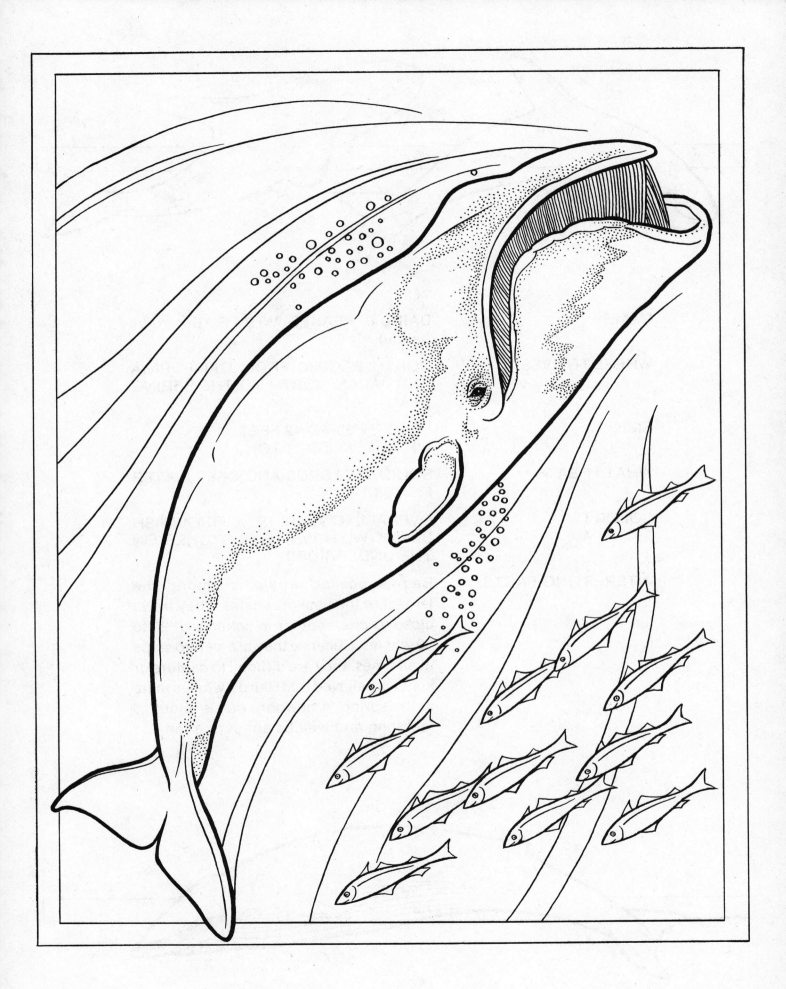

NAME:	BAIRD'S BEAKED WHALE (*Berardius bairdii*)
WHERE IT LIVES:	NORTH PACIFIC FROM CALIFORNIA AND JAPAN NORTH TO THE BERING SEA
SIZE:	LENGTH: 39 TO 42 FEET WEIGHT: 13 TO 14 TONS
WHAT IT EATS:	SQUID, OCTOPUS AND DEEP WATER FISHES
COLOR IT:	OVERALL COLOR IS A BROWNISH BLACK WITH WHITE BLOTCHES ON THE UNDERSIDES
INTERESTING FACTS:	Baird's beaked whale is among the largest of the beaked whales. They travel close to one another in schools of 20 to 30 whales. Because they are alert to ships at all times, they are difficult to capture or kill. It is believed that Baird's whales mate in the spring. A newborn calf is about 15 feet long and weighs about one ton.

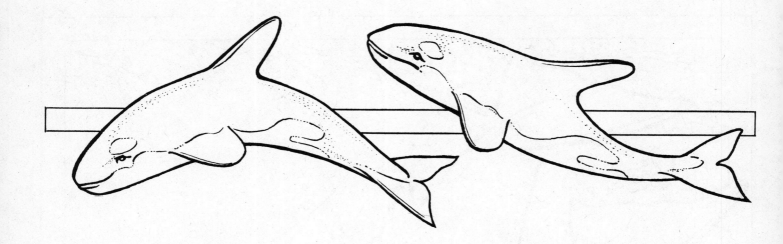

NAME:	FINBACK WHALE (*Balaenoptera physalus*)
WHERE IT LIVES:	ALL OCEANS
SIZE:	LENGTH: 70 TO 76 FEET WEIGHT: 65 TO 70 TONS
WHAT IT EATS:	KRILL (PLANKTONIC ORGANISMS) AND SMALL FISH
INTERESTING FACTS:	The finback whale has a tapered body and powerful muscles which enable it to swim at speeds up to 20 knots (about 23 miles per hour). It is sometimes called the "greyhound of the sea." This, the most common of the baleen whales, usually travels in pods (family groups) of 6 or 7. Because it prefers deep water, it is rarely seen near shore. The female has a calf every other year.

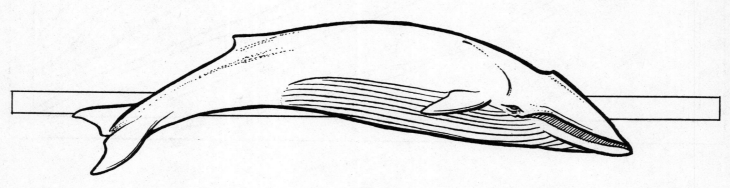

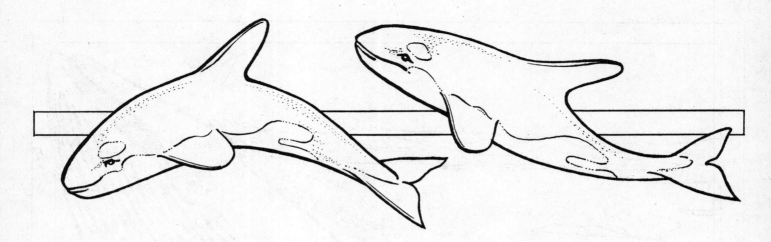

NAME:	BOTTLE-NOSED WHALE (*Hyperoodon ampullatus*)
WHERE IT LIVES:	NORTH ATLANTIC IN THE SUMMER SOUTH TO THE MEDITERRANEAN IN WINTER
SIZE:	LENGTH: 24 TO 29 FEET WEIGHT: 4500 TO 6000 POUNDS
WHAT IT EATS:	SQUID AND CUTTLEFISH
COLOR IT:	GRAYISH TO BLACK ABOVE, YELLOWISH WHITE BELOW WHICH BECOMES LIGHTER WITH AGE
INTERESTING FACTS:	The bottle-nosed whales travel in pods of 4 to 12. They exhibit a certain amount of loyalty and if one member of a pod becomes hurt or wounded, the rest will not desert the wounded member. They have the ability to leap completely out of the water and can dive with great speed. Usually they stay under water from 10 to 20 minutes when feeding, but they are able to stay under for several hours if necessary. Migration is in response to the migration of their prey. New born calves can be seen in Arctic waters during the months of May and June.

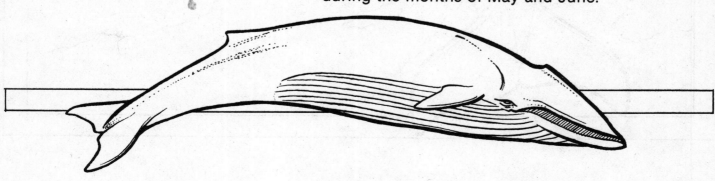

30

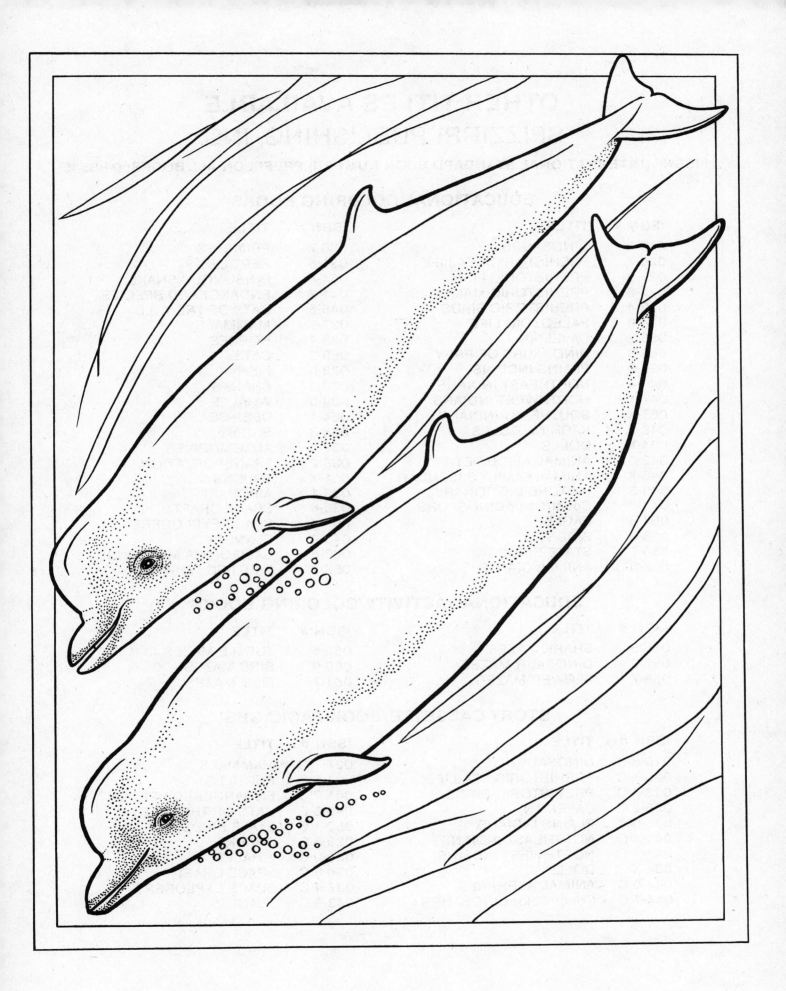

OTHER TITLES AVAILABLE
SPIZZIRRI PUBLISHING, INC.

"ISBN" (INTERNATIONAL STANDARD BOOK NUMBER) PREFIX ON ALL BOOKS: 0-86545-

EDUCATIONAL COLORING BOOKS

ISBN #	TITLE	ISBN #	TITLE
019-6	DINOSAURS	030-7	PRIMATES
020-X	PREHISTORIC SEA LIFE	031-5	REPTILES
021-8	PREHISTORIC FISH	054-4	POISONOUS SNAKES
022-6	PREHISTORIC MAMMALS	041-2	ENDANGERED SPECIES
023-4	PREHISTORIC BIRDS	045-5	CATS OF THE WILD
024-2	PALEOZOIC LIFE	027-7	MAMMALS
055-2	CAVEMAN	068-4	HORSES
063-3	DINOSAURS OF PREY	069-2	CATS
025-0	PLAINS INDIANS	028-5	FISH
040-4	NORTHEAST INDIANS	029-3	SHARKS
047-1	NORTHWEST INDIANS	039-0	WHALES
065-X	SOUTHEAST INDIANS	064-1	DEEP-SEA FISH
046-3	KACHINA DOLLS	035-8	SHIPS
034-X	DOLLS	032-3	AUTOMOBILES
042-0	ANIMAL ALPHABET	038-2	TRANSPORTATION
048-X	ANIMAL FAMILY CALENDAR	051-X	TRUCKS
049-8	PICTURE DICTIONARY	033-1	AIRCRAFT
044-7	Count/Color DINOSAURS	036-6	SPACE CRAFT
067-6	EAGLES	037-4	SPACE EXPLORERS
026-9	BIRDS	043-9	PLANETS
050-1	STATE BIRDS	062-5	CALIFORNIA MISSIONS
066-8	ANIMAL GIANTS	058-2	LAUTREC POSTERS

EDUCATIONAL ACTIVITY/COLORING BOOKS

ISBN #	TITLE	ISBN #	TITLE
056-0	SHARK MAZES	059-5	TURTLE MAZES
057-9	DINOSAUR MAZES	060-9	BIRD MAZES
058-7	FLOWER MAZES	061-7	FISH MAZES

STORY CASSETTE/BOOK PACKAGES

ISBN #	TITLE	ISBN #	TITLE
019-6 C	DINOSAURS	027-7 C	MAMMALS
020-X C	PREHISTORIC SEA LIFE	031-5 C	REPTILES
023-4 C	PREHISTORIC BIRDS	041-2 C	ENDANGERED SPECIES
055-2 C	CAVEMAN	045-5 C	CATS OF THE WILD
025-0 C	PLAINS INDIANS	050-1 C	STATE BIRDS
040-4 C	NORTHEAST INDIANS	029-3 C	SHARKS
047-1 C	NORTHWEST INDIANS	039-0 C	WHALES
034-X C	DOLLS	036-6 C	SPACE CRAFT
042-0 C	ANIMAL ALPHABET	037-4 C	SPACE EXPLORERS
044-7 C	Count/Color DINOSAURS	043-9 C	PLANETS